My United States

Oklahoma

TAMRA B. ORR

Children's Press®
An Imprint of Scholastic Inc.

Content Consultant

James Wolfinger, PhD, Associate Dean and Professor
College of Education, DePaul University, Chicago, Illinois

Library of Congress Cataloging-in-Publication Data
Names: Orr, Tamra, author.
Title: Oklahoma / by Tamra B. Orr.
Description: New York : Children's Press, an imprint of Scholastic, 2018. | Series: A true book | Includes
    bibliographical references and index.
Identifiers: LCCN 2017028547 | ISBN 9780531231708 (library binding) | ISBN 9780531247211 (pbk.)
Subjects: LCSH: Oklahoma—Juvenile literature.
Classification: LCC F694.3 .O77 2018 | DDC 976.6—dc23
LC record available at https://lccn.loc.gov/2017028547

1 2 3 4 5 6 7 8 9 10 R 27 26 25 24 23 22 21 20 19 18

Front cover: Tallgrass Prairie Preserve
Back cover: A shell carving from Craig Mound

Welcome to Oklahoma

Find the Truth!

Everything you are about to read is true **except** for one of the sentences on this page.

Which one is **TRUE**?

T or F Powerful dust storms forced many Oklahoma farmers to leave the state in the 1930s.

T or F Oklahoma's state government is divided into four branches.

Capital: Oklahoma City

Estimated population as of 2016: 3,923,561

Nickname: The Sooner State

Biggest cities: Oklahoma City, Tulsa, Norman

UNITED STATES

Oklahoma

Find the answers in this book.

Contents

THE BIG TRUTH!

Scissor-tailed
flycatcher

What Represents Oklahoma?

Mistletoe

4

Rodeo

3 History

How did Oklahoma become the state it is today?... **25**

4 Culture

What do Oklahomans do for work and fun? **35**

Buffalo

This Is Oklahoma!

COLORADO

KANSAS

Black Mesa

Selman Bat Cave

Cimarron River

Cimarron

National Wrestling Hall of Fame and Museum

Woolaroc Museum and National Preserve

Ozark Mountains

Arkansas River

The Plains Indians and Pioneers Museum

WOODWARD

ENID

OKLAHOMA

Arkansas

TULSA

③

TAHLEQU

② Oklahoma City Zoo

Cherokee Heritage Center

① ROUTE 66

Oklahoma Route 66 Museum

International Rodeo Finals

★ **OKLAHOMA CITY**

National Weather Center

④ Canadian

MCALESTER

Tsa-La-Gi Ancient Village

Wichita Mountains Wildlife Refuge

LAWTON

N W E S

0   60
Miles

Red River

TEXAS

OKLAHOMA
US
66

① Route 66

Route 66 was one of the country's first highways. Over 400 miles (644 kilometers) of the highway go through Oklahoma. Driving down the highway, visitors can see a wild mix of authentic diners, bright neon signs, state-of-the-art museums, and a number of other roadside attractions.

② Oklahoma City Zoo

Oklahoma's biggest zoo offers visitors a chance to experience everything from African plains to tropical jungles. Guests can touch stingrays, see red pandas (pictured), and much more.

③ Woolaroc Museum and Wildlife Preserve

People love to see and take pictures of the many American bison, longhorn cattle (pictured), and elk on this 3,700-acre 1,497-hectare) ranch. The preserve also has a western-themed museum and cowboy lodge.

④ National Weather Center

This is a great place to visit to learn more about Oklahoma's history of huge tornadoes and ground-shaking storms. Visitors can also stop in at the Storm Prediction Center to see weather scientists at work.

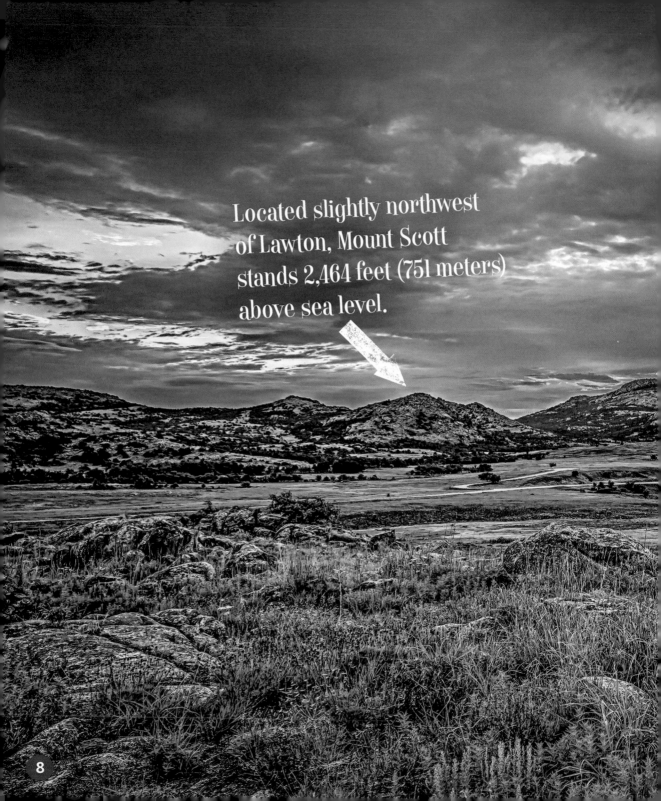

Located slightly northwest of Lawton, Mount Scott stands 2,464 feet (751 meters) above sea level.

Land and Wildlife

Welcome to Oklahoma! A quick look at this state's shape makes it obvious why it is sometimes referred to as the Panhandle State. Oklahoma looks like a large frying pan with a long handle sticking out in the northwest. It is a rich land full of wide-open spaces and beautiful natural scenery, from plains and mountains to **plateaus** and hills.

The Lay of the Land

Oklahoma's Panhandle area is full of flat grasslands, while the middle part of the state is made up of forests, **fertile** soil, and crops of cotton and wheat. The Sandstone Hills in east-central Oklahoma feature thick forests, and farmers use the land to grow corn, fruit, and soybeans. The Arbuckle Mountains in the south are where cattle roam, while the Wichita Mountains in the southwest feature jagged **granite** peaks.

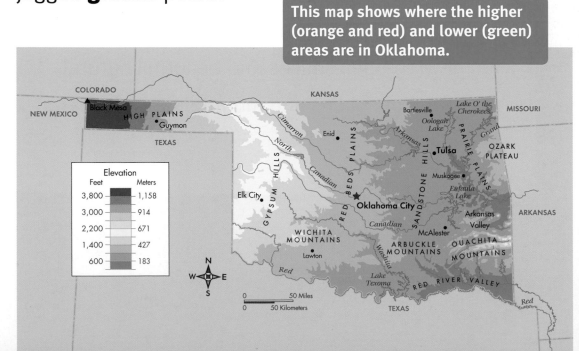

This map shows where the higher (orange and red) and lower (green) areas are in Oklahoma.

"Glass Mountains"

Imagine what would happen if rolling mountains were covered in glass. When the sun hit them, they would light up like mirrors at dawn. Western Oklahoma's Gypsum Hills are almost like that. They are covered in gypsum, a whitish-yellow mineral that often turns into transparent crystals. This has earned the Gypsum Hills the nickname Glass Mountains.

Spanish explorers called the Gypsum Hills "the Shining Mountains."

Oklahoma Wind

"Oklahoma, where the wind comes sweepin' down the plain, and the wavin' wheat can sure smell sweet when the wind comes right behind the rain." These song lyrics sum up Oklahoma's weather perfectly. The state is known for its wind. Sometimes the wind brings a welcome breeze to hot, dry summers. Other times it transforms into Oklahoma's many thunderstorms or tornadoes. In winters, the wind brings a sharp chill to the air and sometimes even a blizzard.

MAXIMUM TEMPERATURE
120°F

MINIMUM TEMPERATURE
-31°F

Storm researchers drive toward a tornado in Katie, Oklahoma.

Beavers Bend State Park is home to many types of trees, including many that grow up from the water.

A Land of Trees

Oklahoma is the perfect place to see a huge variety of trees all growing in the same place. It has more than 130 different types, including familiar ones such as pine, maple, and oak. Less common species include sweet gum, pecan, dogwood, and redbud. Cypress trees grow tall in Oklahoma, and waterways are lined by willow, cedar, and hackberry trees. Indian blanket, the state wildflower, grows in pastures next to colorful sunflowers, black-eyed Susans, and purple **thistles**.

An Abundance of Wildlife

With its thick forests and open plains, Oklahoma is the perfect place for many animals to live. Forests harbor deer, foxes, raccoons, and squirrels. The plains are home to herds of grazing cattle as well as armadillos, coyotes, and prairie dogs. Hawks and owls patrol the skies looking for a tasty meal below. Lakes and rivers have ducks and geese, while the air is filled with the songs of meadowlarks, warblers, and blackbirds.

An armadillo can roll up into a ball to protect itself from enemies.

An adult bison can weigh up to 2,200 pounds (998 kilograms).

Bringing Back Bison

Hundreds of years ago, one of the most common animals to roam Oklahoma's plains was the bison (buffalo). But by the end of the 1800s, there were only a few hundred bison left in the entire country. People had simply hunted too many of them. To keep the species from going **extinct**, people began working to protect bison. The first wildlife preserve for bison was established in Oklahoma in 1907. Thanks to this and other organizations, there are about 350,000 bison in the United States today.

Oklahoma's state capitol has an oil well underneath its grounds! The well is called Petunia Number One, and it has produced oil for more than 43 years.

STATE OF OKLAHO

CHAPTER 2

Government

Before Oklahoma became a state, its capital was a town called Guthrie. But by 1907, when Oklahoma gained statehood, Oklahoma City had grown to become the center of business and culture. Many of the city's residents believed that it should become the new state's capital. Oklahoma's people voted on the issue, and the state government officially moved to Oklahoma City in 1917. It has been centered there ever since.

Three Branches

Oklahoma's government is divided into three branches: legislative, executive, and judicial. The legislative branch makes the state's laws. It is made up of a Senate and a House of Representatives. Laws are carried out by the executive branch, which is led by the governor. The judicial branch enforces the laws. This branch consists of a system of courts and is led by the state supreme court.

OKLAHOMA'S STATE GOVERNMENT

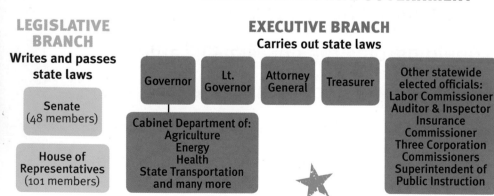

LEGISLATIVE BRANCH
Writes and passes state laws

Senate
(48 members)

House of Representatives
(101 members)

EXECUTIVE BRANCH
Carries out state laws

Governor | Lt. Governor | Attorney General | Treasurer

Cabinet Department of:
Agriculture
Energy
Health
State Transportation
and many more

Other statewide elected officials:
Labor Commissioner
Auditor & Inspector
Insurance Commissioner
Three Corporation Commissioners
Superintendent of Public Instruction

JUDICIAL BRANCH
Enforces state laws

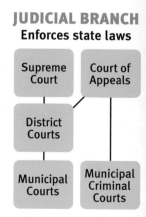

Supreme Court | Court of Appeals

District Courts

Municipal Courts | Municipal Criminal Courts

Bill John Baker has served as the Principal Chief of the Cherokee Nation since 2011.

Native American Government

Oklahoma is home to many Native American groups. In addition to following U.S. and state laws, each of these groups has its own tribal government and legal system. Like the state government, most tribal governments are often divided into branches. For example, there might be an executive branch led by an official called a chief or a tribal council that serves as a legislature.

Oklahoma in the National Government

Each state elects officials to represent it in the U.S. Congress. Like every state, Oklahoma has two senators. The U.S. House of Representatives relies on a state's population to determine its numbers. Oklahoma has five representatives in the House.

Every four years, states vote on the next U.S. president. Each state is granted a number of electoral votes based on its number of members of Congress. With two senators and five representatives, Oklahoma has seven electoral votes.

2 senators and 5 representatives

7 electoral votes

Oklahoma has an average number of electoral votes.

The People of Oklahoma

Elected officials in Oklahoma represent a population with a range of interests, lifestyles, and backgrounds.

Ethnicity (2016 estimates)

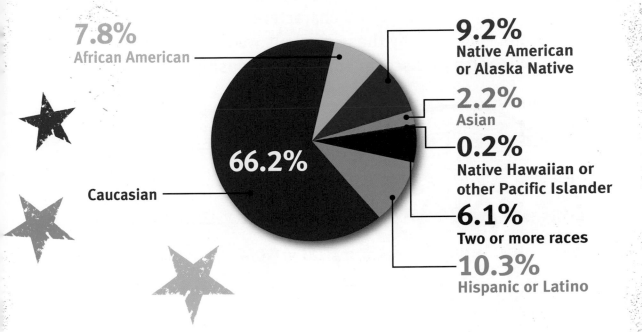

7.8%
African American

9.2%
Native American or Alaska Native

2.2%
Asian

0.2%
Native Hawaiian or other Pacific Islander

66.2%
Caucasian

6.1%
Two or more races

10.3%
Hispanic or Latino

66%
own their homes.

10%
speak a language other than English at home.

66%
live in cities.

87%
of the population graduated from high school.

24%
of the population have a degree beyond high school.

21

What Represents Oklahoma?

States choose specific animals, plants, and objects to represent the values and characteristics of the land and its people. Find out why these symbols were chosen to represent Oklahoma or discover surprising curiosities about them.

Seal

Oklahoma's state seal features a five-pointed star. Each point represents a major Native American group. The five groups represented are the Cherokee, the Chickasaw, the Choctaw, the Creek, and the Seminole.

Flag

The Oklahoma state flag was adopted on April 2, 1925. It features many symbols of the state's Native American heritage. The flag's background is the same shade as the flag that Choctaw soldiers carried during the Civil War (1861–1865). A buffalo skin Osage shield is in the middle, with eagle feathers hanging from it. The pipe and olive branch are symbols of peace.

Scissor-Tailed Flycatcher

STATE BIRD
This bird is named for the long feathers that extend from its tail. It lives throughout Oklahoma.

Mistletoe

STATE FLORAL EMBLEM
Mistletoe has been an official symbol of Oklahoma since 1893, years before the Oklahoma Territory became a state.

Milk

STATE BEVERAGE
Oklahoma's dairy cows produce about 700 million pounds (317.5 million kg) of milk each year.

Redbud

STATE TREE
This tree's bright-pink flowers are a common sight across the state every spring.

Buffalo

STATE ANIMAL
An adult buffalo can measure up to 6 feet (1.8 m) tall at the shoulder.

Honeybee

STATE INSECT
Without bees, Oklahoma's beautiful wildflowers would not be able to reproduce.

About 15,000 Cherokees were forced out of their homes during the Trail of Tears. Approximately 4,000 of them died along the way.

CHAPTER 3

History

When spring comes to Oklahoma, the scent of wild onions fills the air. For many of the area's Native Americans, this early green plant means it's time to honor the past. Traditionally, the onions are picked, cleaned, chopped, and boiled, and then served with scrambled eggs. The meal is offered at local churches and community centers to remember a time when Native Americans on the Trail of Tears relied on spring plants like this to survive each day.

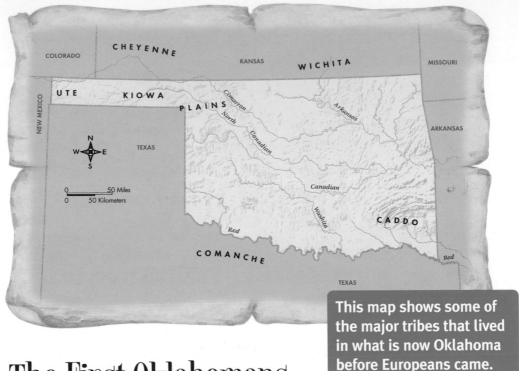

This map shows some of the major tribes that lived in what is now Oklahoma before Europeans came.

The First Oklahomans

Oklahoma has been home to Native American peoples such as the Caddo, Ute, and Kiowa for about 10,000 years. Spanish explorers came to the area in the 1500s. By the 1700s, France and Spain were battling over who controlled the land. Oklahoma finally became part of the United States when President Thomas Jefferson bought it from France as a piece of the Louisiana Purchase in 1803.

Into Indian Territory

In 1830, the Indian Removal Act was passed, forcing many Native Americans in the southeast to move west. Their long and difficult journey became known as the Trail of Tears. Many of them settled in Oklahoma. Soon, the area became known as Indian Territory. By the end of the 19th century, Oklahoma had more than 30 Native American groups living in it. But when more new settlers started moving westward, land was once again taken from Native Americans and given to white residents.

Caddos built homes by covering wooden frames with dried grass.

Sooners and Boomers

On April 22, 1889, thousands of people lined up in Oklahoma, waiting for a pistol to fire. When it did, wagons and horses loaded down with people and belongings rushed across these "unassigned lands." Each family claimed a **homestead**. A few people, however, had snuck in earlier and hid until it was time to claim their land. These "sooners" were Oklahoma's first white settlers. (Those who left after the pistol fired were called boomers.)

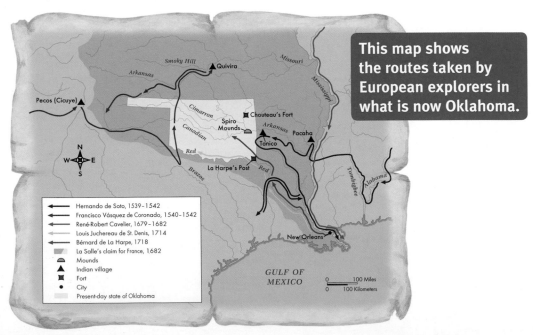

This map shows the routes taken by European explorers in what is now Oklahoma.

Boomers rush into Oklahoma to stake claims on homesteads in 1889

Becoming a State

When Oklahoma became the country's 46th state in 1907, the Native Americans living in the region immediately became U.S. citizens. Many were not happy about this change. They wanted to remain a separate state called Sequoyah so that they could keep their own governments. Now that Oklahoma was a part of the United States, more and more people began moving there. Soon, the state was a booming center of agriculture.

Oklahoma's Oil

Oklahoma's first oil well was discovered in 1897 in Bartlesville. More followed, bringing nationwide attention and curious investors. Within a few years, Tulsa was being called the Oil Capital of the World. Some of the state's oil wells were giants, producing millions of barrels of oil a year. This business brought tremendous wealth to some Oklahomans.

Timeline of Oklahoma Events

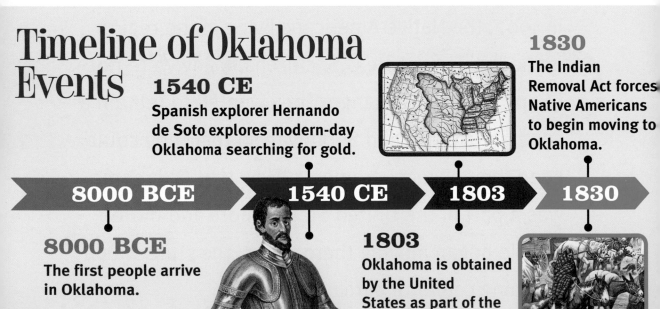

1540 CE
Spanish explorer Hernando de Soto explores modern-day Oklahoma searching for gold.

1830
The Indian Removal Act forces Native Americans to begin moving to Oklahoma.

8000 BCE   **1540 CE**   **1803**   **1830**

8000 BCE
The first people arrive in Oklahoma.

1803
Oklahoma is obtained by the United States as part of the Louisiana Purchase.

The Dust Bowl

In the 1930s, **drought** made Oklahoma's land incredibly dry. Combined with the state's powerful winds, this was a recipe for huge dust storms. Looking out their windows, all farmers could see was swirling dust. Everything was covered in layers of dirt. Nothing could grow. The drought continued for almost a decade, making farming almost impossible. Many "Okies" fled the area during this period.

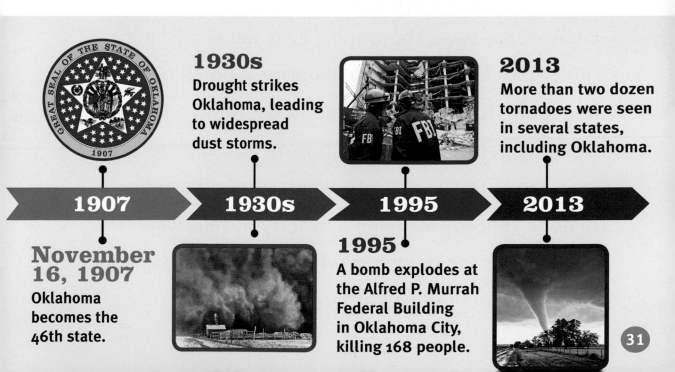

1930s
Drought strikes Oklahoma, leading to widespread dust storms.

2013
More than two dozen tornadoes were seen in several states, including Oklahoma.

1907

1930s

1995

2013

November 16, 1907
Oklahoma becomes the 46th state.

1995
A bomb explodes at the Alfred P. Murrah Federal Building in Oklahoma City, killing 168 people.

Today, a national memorial and a museum in Oklahoma City honor the victims of the bombing.

A National Tragedy

On April 19, 1995, the world's eyes were watching downtown Oklahoma City in horror. A bomb placed in a rental truck outside the Alfred P. Murrah Federal Building had exploded, destroying the building. It was one of the worst terrorist attacks in the nation's history. Timothy McVeigh and Terry Nichols were arrested for the bombing, which killed 168 people and injured more than 650 others.

Cherokee Chief: Wilma Mankiller

Wilma Mankiller (1945–2010) was born in Oklahoma to a Cherokee family. Her life changed dramatically when she was in a serious car accident. It was a long and difficult recovery, but she was determined to make it. In 1983, Mankiller became the deputy chief of Oklahoma's Cherokee Nation. Two years later, she became the first woman to become tribal chief, a position she held for eight years. She worked to improve Native American health care and education. For her efforts, she was awarded the Presidential Medal of Freedom in 1998.

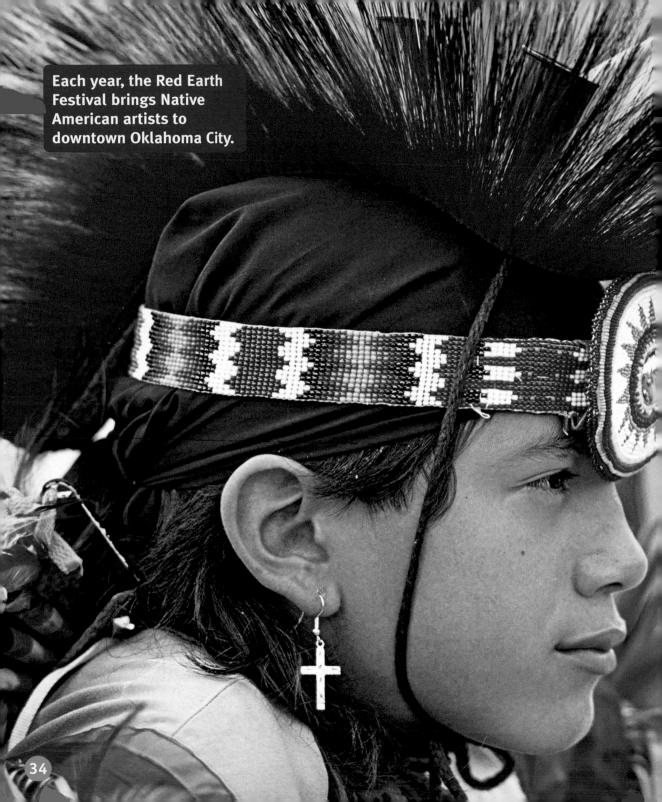

Each year, the Red Earth Festival brings Native American artists to downtown Oklahoma City.

CHAPTER

Culture

Oklahoma attracts people from all over the country. Some just come to visit, while others settle down there. Many people come to soak in the state's rich Native American history. Some come to experience the beautiful scenery and spend time on one of the hundreds of lakes. Others want to connect to their inner cowboys and cowgirls. For example, a visit to the Oklahoma City Stockyards offers everything from exciting cattle auctions to action-packed rodeos to delicious steakhouses. Yee-haw!

Oklahoma football fans look forward to games between the state's two biggest teams: the Sooners and the Cowboys.

Sports

Oklahomans love to cheer on the Oklahoma City Thunder basketball team. Oklahoma's college teams are also a major draw for sports fans. The University of Oklahoma Sooners, the Cowboys and Cowgirls of Oklahoma State University, and the University of Tulsa Golden Hurricanes all participate in a variety of sports. Football, basketball, and baseball are some of the most popular. Many fans enjoy cheering for these colleges' golfers, wrestlers, and other athletes.

Time to Celebrate

It is almost impossible to find a weekend without a big celebration somewhere in Oklahoma. Rodeos are held all summer in multiple cities. The 101 Wild West Rodeo in Ponca City has been going for more than 50 years and features steer roping, bareback riding, and barrel racing. In Oklahoma City, many people catch the Jazz Fest or go to the town of Grove for the American Heritage Music Festival. The Chisholm Trail & Crawfish Festival in Yukon is a great place to get a taste of local Oklahoma flavors.

A young rider participates in the 2017 International Finals Youth Rodeo in Shawnee.

Top Oklahoma Industries

Oklahoma's people work in a wide range of industries. Many have jobs dealing with energy, whether it's oil and natural gas or wind energy, which has recently been making a big impact on the state. Others work in technology. Big companies such as Google and IBM have offices in Oklahoma. The U.S. military is also a big employer. Tinker Air Force Base in Oklahoma City is the world's largest aircraft-maintenance complex and military-aviation **logistics** center.

Oil workers are often called roughnecks.

Shifting Nation, Shifting Jobs

For many decades, agriculture, manufacturing, and mining have been staples of Oklahoma's economy. But in recent years, Oklahoma has focused on other businesses, including medical research, health, and **aeronautical** education and training. One of the fastest-growing industries in Oklahoma is that of specialty trade contractors. These include plumbers, electricians, and heating and air-conditioning technicians—the people everyone needs on a regular basis. Jobs in all areas of health care are also on the rise.

Grab a Plate

When it comes to food, Oklahoma is known for two things: barbecue and deep-fried fare. Chicken-fried steak smothered in gravy is a favorite. So are steaks and deep-fried catfish. On the side, you will find deep-fried okra, and almost every meal comes with generous servings of corn bread and grits.

  ## Cowboy Caviar

Ask an adult to help you!

Some people like this as a side dish or a salad, while others use it for dipping their chips. It is a common sight at Oklahoma potluck dinners!

Ingredients

- 2 cans (14 ounces each) black-eyed peas, rinsed and drained
- 1 can (14 ounces) black beans, rinsed and drained
- 1 can (14 ounces) fresh-cut corn
- 1 1/2 cups chopped tomatoes
- 1 medium red, orange, or yellow bell pepper
- 3/4 cup chopped red onion
- 1/2 cup chopped cilantro
- 1/2 cup Italian salad dressing
- Salt and pepper

Directions

Combine all the ingredients except the dressing in a bowl and mix well. Drizzle the dressing over the mixture and toss until well combined. Add salt and pepper to taste. Let the mixture sit at least 20 minutes before serving.

There are many great places to camp and enjoy the outdoors in Oklahoma.

The Wonders of Oklahoma

Whether a person comes to Oklahoma to enjoy the scenery, take a road trip, or connect with a part of American history, it is sure to be an adventure. It is little surprise that so many people rushed into this land so many years ago and continue to do so today. Oklahomans know their state is rich in everything that makes this country an amazing and beautiful place. ★

Famous People

Sam Walton

(1918–1992) was the founder of Walmart and one of the most successful businessmen in U.S. history. He was born in Kingfisher.

Mickey Mantle

(1931–1995) was one of the most famous baseball players in history. He played for the New York Yankees from 1951 to 1968 and was inducted into the National Baseball Hall of Fame in 1974. He was born in Spavinaw.

Phil McGraw

(1950–) is an author and television personality who is best known as the host of the TV show *Dr. Phil*. He was born in Vinita.

Ron Howard

(1954–) was a child actor in *The Andy Griffith Show*. He later went on to star in the TV series *Happy Days* and to be a successful Hollywood director. He was born in Duncan.

Reba McEntire

(1955–) is a singer, songwriter, and actress who is known as the queen of country. She was born in McAlester.

Brad Pitt

(1963–) is an award-winning actor who has starred in such films as *Ocean's Eleven* and *Moneyball*. He was born in Shawnee.

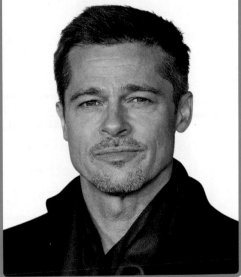

Kristin Chenoweth

(1968–) is a television, movie, and Broadway actress who began singing as a child in her church and in school plays. She was born in Broken Arrow.

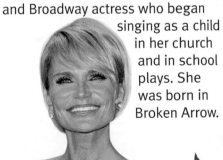

Carrie Underwood

(1983–) is a singer, songwriter, and actress who won the fourth season of *American Idol* in 2005. She was born on a farm in Muskogee.

Did You Know That ...

Oklahoma has more human-made lakes than any other state in the country.

The world's first parking meter was installed in Oklahoma City on July 16, 1935.

Beaver is the site of the annual World Cow Chip Throwing Championship. Each April, people compete to see how far these pieces of dried cow dung can be thrown.

Okmulgee is known for its annual Pecan Festival. The city features the world's largest pecan pie, pecan cookie, and pecan brownie.

In Bristow, it is illegal to serve water to someone in a restaurant unless one peanut in a shell is also served. If this rule is overlooked, a fine of up to $5.00 can be issued.

Oklahoma has an official state meal: fried okra, squash, corn bread, BBQ pork, biscuits, sausage, gravy, grits, corn, strawberries, chicken-fried steak, pecan pie, and black-eyed peas.

Did you find the truth?

(T) Powerful dust storms forced many Oklahoma farmers to leave the state in the 1930s.

(F) Oklahoma's state government is divided into four branches.

Resources

Books

Nonfiction

Dillard, Sheri. *What's Great About Oklahoma?* Minneapolis: Lerner, 2015.

Maine, Tyler. *Oklahoma*. Mankato, MN: Capstone Press, 2016.

Saylor-Marchant, Linda. *Oklahoma*. New York: Children's Press, 2008.

Fiction

Rawls, Wilson. *Where the Red Fern Grows*. Garden City, NY: Doubleday, 1961.

Steinbeck, John. *The Grapes of Wrath*. New York: Viking, 1939.

Visit this Scholastic website for more information on Oklahoma:
★ www.factsfornow.scholastic.com
Enter the keyword **Oklahoma**